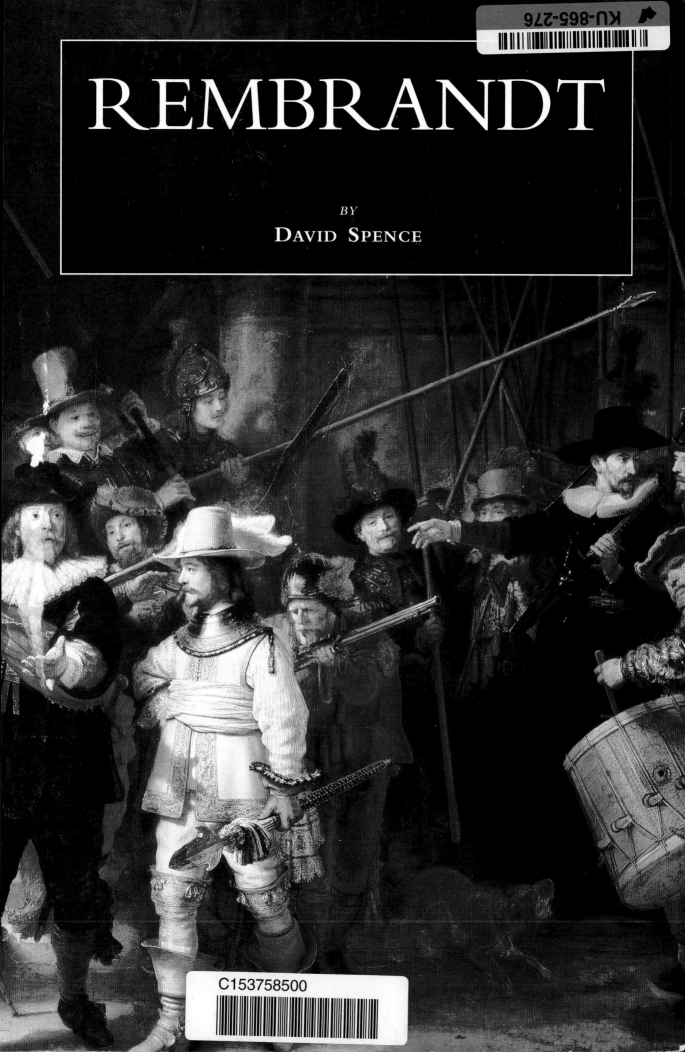

REMBRANDT

BY
DAVID SPENCE

THE WORLD IN THE 1650S

What was the world like when Rembrandt was alive? European powers were expanding their influence far and wide, with English and Dutch settlements in North America beginning to rival those of the Spanish and Portuguese in South America and the Caribbean. European trade in the East was growing with the important spice trade in the East Indies. In England there was civil war. King Charles I was executed as Oliver Cromwell's Parliamentary Army swept to power. The United Provinces of the Netherlands had finally shaken the domination of Spain by 1648 and was becoming one of the wealthiest countries in the world thanks to the strength of its seaborne empire and Dutch East India Company. In the 1650s Russia's armies invaded the forests of China whose ruling Ming family dynasty was at an end. Japan's ruling Shogun military dictatorship expelled all foreigners from the country; Japan's borders were to be closed for over 200 years.

SHAH JAHAN & THE TAJ MAHAL

This huge and magnificent white marble building is a tomb, built in 1631 in memory of Mumtaz Mahal, wife of the Moghul emperor Shah Jahan (shown above). The building is inlaid with many precious stones and is a good example of the riches of India which drew the English traders in the 1600s.

RENÉ DESCARTES

The French philosopher and mathematician who lived during the first half of the 17th century is considered to have founded modern philosophy. His statement 'Cogito ergo sum' ('*I think therefore I am*') has become famous and often quoted.

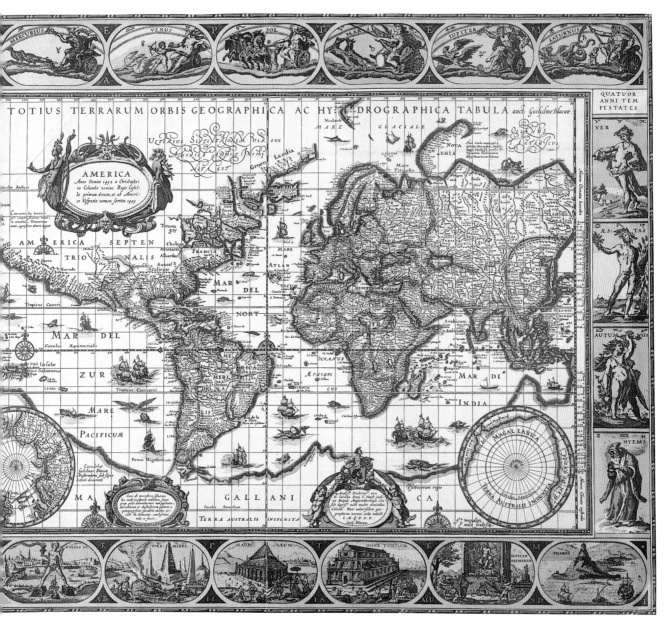

MAP OF THE WORLD, 1650

By 1650 the shape of the world was largely known. The great southern land mass of Australia was yet to be encountered, and the polar regions were still unmapped, yet the Dutch were already proficient map-makers using the knowledge gained from their considerable merchant and navy fleets which travelled to many parts of the globe. By 1650 New York, or New Amsterdam as it was then known, had a population of about 1500.

BLOOD CIRCULATION

The English doctor William Harvey published an account of blood circulation in the human body. His work, from the 1620s to his death in 1657, enabled important advances in medicine. Harvey made meticulous drawings, like wiring diagrams, which demonstrated how blood circulated through the arteries and returned to the heart via the veins. His ideas were slow to gain acceptance because they contradicted the thinking of the day.

THE WORLD OF REMBRANDT

'*You can buy anything you want, you are free, and you are safe*' said the French philosopher Descartes about Amsterdam. This was the world in which Rembrandt worked and lived, being described as 'Rembrandt van Rijn, merchant, of Amsterdam' on a document dated 1 November 1642. The town was inhabited by people from many different cultures and religions: Catholics, Jews, Calvinists and Lutherans were free to worship as they pleased. The wealthy merchants of Amsterdam were university-educated with a knowledge of languages and an appreciation of art. Rembrandt was born in Leiden, taking up residence in Amsterdam in 1633. At this time the Northern Provinces, including Holland, had become independent of Spain although the Netherlands was not to win complete independence until 1648. Holland was prosperous and cosmopolitan, and could be said to be entering into its 'golden age'.

SELF-PORTRAIT, *(detail)* 1640

This portrait was painted when Rembrandt was 34 years old. By this age he had established himself as a painter, was married and had bought a house. His marriage to Saskia van Uylenburgh was considered a good one. Rembrandt, the son of a miller, had married the daughter of a mayor; she would have brought a good dowry with her. Rembrandt purchased his own house in the Breestraat for the sum of 13,000 guilders, although he did not pay for the house immediately and was slow in making payments.

VIEW ON THE AMSTEL LOOKING TOWARDS AMSTERDAM, *Jacob Isaakszoon van Ruisdael*

Rembrandt moved to Amsterdam after his father's death in 1630. Amsterdam was the most important town in the Dutch Republic, its growth based on the shipping trade, particularly wood and grain from the Baltic ports. The foundation of the Dutch East India Company in 1602 strengthened the Dutch domination of world trade and navigation at sea, with the trade in spices and Eastern goods bringing fabulous wealth to the town. Many of the inhabitants of Amsterdam participated in 'ships' share poker'. By investing in shares it was possible for all the citizens to gamble a little and make some money, or if the ship foundered, to lose their stake.

PURITAN FASHION

The clothes of the burghers of Amsterdam were plain and straightforward. As in this example, the majority of Rembrandt's portraits of well-to-do men and women show them dressed in black clothes with white collar and cuffs. Sometimes the women wear a white cap and the more flamboyant men wear decorative lace trimmings on their shoes. Black and white was the uniform of the day, just as the suit is to us today. The fashion moved across the Atlantic to America with the Dutch settlers.

THE MILLER'S SON

Rembrandt was born in 1606 to Cornelia and Harmen Gerritsz van Rijn. His father was a prosperous malt-miller who supplied the local beer industry. Two windmills dominated the view from the family house in Leiden. The town was an important centre for textiles and Leiden University was becoming well known in Europe.

A REMBRANDT TULIP

The Dutch have been famous for their tulips since the plants were first brought to Europe from the Middle East in the sixteenth-century. Dutch flower painting often included tulips, particularly the variety which has come to be known as the Rembrandt Tulip with its striped colours.

ENGLAND - ANTHONY VAN DYCK

Charles I of England out Hunting
A pupil of the famous Dutch artist Rubens in his home town of Antwerp, Anthony van Dyck moved to England and won the position of court painter to Charles I in 1632. Van Dyck's painting captured the refinement and elegance of the English aristocracy. Charles was a great patron of the arts, bestowing on him the title Sir Anthony van Dyck.

FRANCE - GEORGES DE LA TOUR

Mary Magdalen
The obsession with light and shade which fills Georges de la Tour's painting is in the tradition of 'baroque' which dominated much of European art. However, many famous French artists of the time, such as Poussin and Lorrain, returned to classicism.

SPAIN - DIEGO VELÁZQUEZ

Las Meninas
Court painter to the King of Spain, Velázquez portrays the world of Spanish royalty with ruthless naturalism in the tradition of the Italian artist Caravaggio whose work impressed him so much. At the centre of the painting is the Infanta Margarita Teresa, daughter of King Philip IV. The painting's title means 'Maids of Honour'.

ITALY - ARTEMISIA GENTILESCHI

Judith Slaying Holofernes
Artemisia Gentileschi's picture exemplifies Italian baroque. The female artist's realistic depiction is made more powerful by dramatic lighting and movement. It was unusual for women to be artists in the 17th century. They were excluded from studying the human form in life classes and as a result were more likely to execute flower paintings than full blooded narratives like this.

THE ART OF HIS DAY

$\mathcal{E}$uropean painting became dominated by realism during the 17th century.

This was later to become known as the Baroque period. Catholic countries were influenced by Italian art, full of movement and drama, while the Northern Protestant countries such as the United Provinces of the Netherlands mirrored nature. In general, however, artists depicted people and events in a natural way, concerned with the depiction of light, form and colour as in real life. Art in the Netherlands flourished during this period more than any other. Three of the greatist artists of the 17th century came from the Netherlands. Peter Paul Rubens worked in the Catholic controlled Flemish town of Antwerp; Rembrandt in Amsterdam; Jan Vermeer in Delft near The Hague.

THE NETHERLANDS - JAN VERMEER

Girl with a Pearl Earring (detail) Little is known about Vermeer's life. We do not even know whether he ever travelled outside his native land to learn about art. He painted people and domestic settings with great skill and detail but his paintings are best known for their sense of stillness and calm, qualities seemingly impossible to capture in paint. In this picture the young girl looks back at the viewer, frozen for a moment, as if only a glance has been exchanged across a room.

THE LIFE OF REMBRANDT

~1606~
Rembrandt van Rijn born
in Leiden on 15 July

~1621~
Becomes a pupil of the
artist Jacob van
Swannenburgh

~1624~
Studies with the artist
Pieter Lastman in
Amsterdam

~1625~
Rembrandt sets up
studio in Leiden

~1630~
Rembrandt's father dies

~1632~
Rembrandt undertakes
several commissions in
Amsterdam and The Hague
including *The Anatomy
Lesson of Dr Tulp*

~1633~
Sets up home in
Amsterdam lodging with
Hendrick van Uylenburgh,
Uncle of Saskia van
Uylenburgh

~1634~
Marries Saskia and
becomes a citizen
of Amsterdam

~1635~
The couple move to a
rented house in the
Nieuwe Doelenstraat.
Rombertus is born but
dies 2 months later

~1638~
Birth of Cornelia, who
dies after a month

SASKIA, 1633

Only one recorded portrait of Saskia
survives. This silverpoint was made by
Rembrandt on his betrothal to his wife.
Rembrandt wrote underneath *'This is
drawn after my wife, when she was twenty-one
years old, the third day after our betrothal - the
eighth of June, 1633'*. No other portrait of
Saskia, or of his women friends later in
life, has been identified although it is
probable that they appear many times in
his pictures as likenesses. Saskia's loss of
her first three children was not an
uncommon experience at the time. Infant
mortality was very high, babies being
especially vulnerable to infections which
were untreatable. Saskia's death deeply affected Rembrandt, who was
working on the big commission for the civic guard (now known as
The Night Watch) at the time. The features of the little girl in the
painting (shown on page 22) appear strangely like those of his wife.

SASKIA WITH ROMBERTUS, *(detail)* 1635/36

The first child born to Saskia and
Rembrandt was a boy whom they named
Rombertus, after Saskia's father rather than
the custom of the day which was to name
the first born son after the father's father.
The baby was baptised in December 1635
but died shortly afterwards.

WOMAN AT AN OPEN DOOR, 1656/57

Although no painting is officially
credited as depicting Hendrickje
Stoffels, she is thought to be the
model for *Woman at an Open
Door*. Rembrandt and Hendrickje
lived as a married couple and
in 1654 they had a daughter,
named Cornelia. Hendrickje
was summoned to appear before
the local church council who
accused her of committing the acts
of a prostitute and barred her from
communion. Despite this the four
(Rembrandt, Hendrickje, Titus and
Cornelia) lived together happily
in their house in the Breestraat.
Rembrandt draws attention to
Hendrickje's status as common-law wife by painting a ring on her
hand and a cord, on which hangs another ring, around her neck.

FAMILY & FRIENDS

Rembrandt was one of nine children, five of whom died when young. His success as a painter in his late twenties was mirrored by rapid social progress when he married Saskia van Uylenburgh who brought with her a substantial dowry. Life must have seemed good to the young couple but they were to suffer the loss of three children. The first, Rombertus, was born in 1635 but survived only two months; Cornelia, born in 1638, survived just one month; and a second daughter born in 1640, also named Cornelia, lived but a few weeks. In September 1641 a son was born and they named him Titus. He was to grow strong and survive but tragically Saskia never fully recovered from the ordeal and died just nine months later in June 1642, leaving Rembrandt a widower with a son to bring up.

TITUS, *(detail)* c1657

Rembrandt's son Titus survived into adulthood. When his mother died Rembrandt employed a housekeeper named Geertje Dircx to help with Titus's upbringing. Rembrandt fell out with Geertje and in 1649 turned his attention to the younger Hendrickje Stoffels, who cared for Titus in the subsequent years. Titus received art lessons from his father but he displayed no obvious inclination to follow in his father's footsteps. In 1655 Rembrandt made his house over to Titus as financial pressures mounted but was declared insolvent in 1656. By 1660 Titus and Hendrickje had set up an art dealing business which in turn employed Rembrandt, an arrangement designed to protect him from creditors. When Titus died in 1668, a year before his father, he left a wife and a six month old daughter named Titia.

FAMILY & FAMILIAR FACES

The picture above is a detail from *Belshazzar's Feast* c1635 (see page 25) and bears a strong resemblance to Saskia, as shown below from the silverpoint portrait, dated 1633 (see page 8).

*R*embrandt needed inspiration for the characters in his paintings when they were not commissioned portraits. Many of the biblical and mythological scenes may have been sketched out in his mind but when it came to the detail, Rembrandt needed to paint from life. His nearest and dearest were often called on to serve as models, dressed for the part in costumes and posing in his studio. Rembrandt's first wife, Saskia, can be recognised time and again in many different guises. Geertje Dircx, his partner after the death of Saskia, took on the role of model for a while but after they parted Hendrickje Stoffels began to appear in the paintings.

SUSANNA AND THE ELDERS, 1647

This painting portrays the story from the Apocrypha of the planned seduction of Susanna (Hebrew for Lily, meaning purity) by two elders of the community. As Susanna bathes the two men surprise her and say *'…consent unto us and live with us. If thou wilt not, we will bear witness against thee, that a young man was with thee…'*. Susanna spurned their advances so they made their false charge of adultery and Susanna was condemned to death. Daniel proved them liars and they were executed in her place. Rembrandt painted the picture in 1647, five years after Geertje Dircx had moved into his house.

The face of Geertje was used to represent Susanna, but her affair with Rembrandt ended unhappily for her. Some time around 1648 the young Hendrickje Stoffels joined the Rembrandt household and his attentions turned to her. Geertje and Rembrandt separated in anger. It is evident that she had expected to marry Rembrandt because she later sued him for breach of promise and alimony payments. Geertje pawned jewellery that had belonged to Saskia and in revenge Rembrandt arranged for her to be locked up in the workhouse for 12 years.

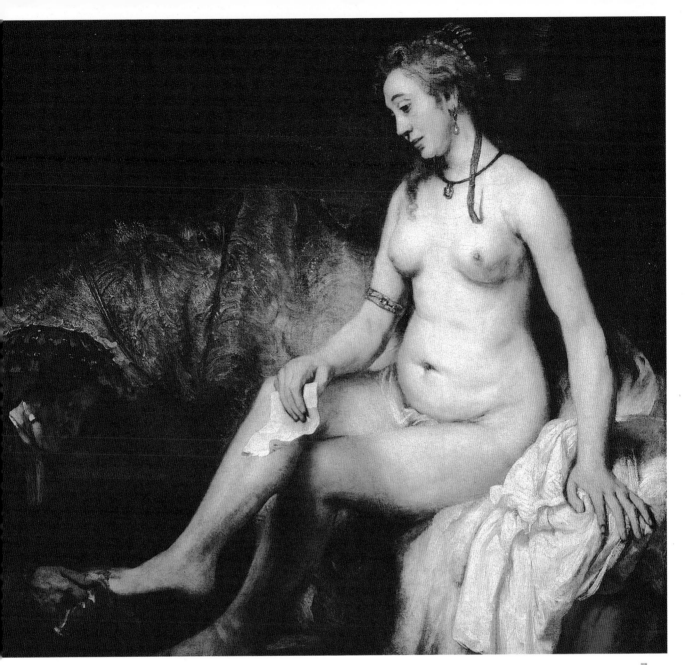

BATHSHEBA WITH KING DAVID'S LETTER, 1654

Another biblical scene, this time from the Book of Samuel, describes how King David commits adultery with Uriah's wife Bathsheba. Bathsheba becomes pregnant as a result so David engineers Uriah's death. A story popular with artists, Rembrandt uses the scene to concentrate on the depiction of the female form.

The face of Bathsheba bears a strong resemblance to those depicted in other paintings during the 1650s, when Hendrickje Stoffels was Rembrandt's common-law wife. It may be no coincidence that this picture, telling the story of a pregnant Bathsheba, was painted in the year that Hendrickje was carrying Rembrandt's daughter.

THE LIFE OF REMBRANDT

~1640~

Birth of second daughter Cornelia who dies after three weeks. Death of Rembrandt's mother

~1641~

Birth of son Titus

~1642~

Saskia dies and is buried at the Oude Kerk. Geertje Dircx joins the household as housekeeper and nanny for Titus

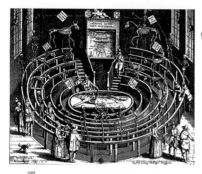

THEATRE OF ANATOMY AT LEIDEN

The study of anatomy was advanced by the dissection of corpses. It was permissible to dissect the corpses of executed criminals but this was possible only a few times a year. When a dissection did take place large crowds of students and sightseers gathered, paying for the privilege of watching the spectacle.

No records of any diaries kept by Rembrandt exist today and only a few letters survive but the chronology of his life is well understood thanks to a great deal of painstaking research by many Rembrandt scholars. Rembrandt's family were millers and he grew up in Leiden with his parents, brothers and younger sister in a small house facing the river next to the family windmill. He went to university at 14 but decided that he wanted to pursue a career as a painter and was apprenticed to the studio of Jacob van Swannenburgh. The apprentice had to master drawing, the art of mixing colours, the theory of perspective and how to imitate the style of his master - even to better it - but not to be original.

Having done this Rembrandt could become a member of an artist's guild and sell paintings in his own right. He moved to Amsterdam and despite the fact that he did not appear to establish himself with the artist's guild, his work became very much in demand. Rembrandt van Rijn, artist, made a good marriage to Saskia van Uylenburgh whose inheritance should have set them up for life.

HAPPY FAMILIES

For a time Rembrandt, Saskia and Titus were a family, but Saskia died not long after Titus' birth. Rembrandt had to bring up the little boy, aided initially by Geertje Dircx and later by Hendrickje Stoffels, in the roles of nurse, housekeeper and 'partner'. He made many sketches of the domestic scenes around him; young children as they were coaxed to eat; as they had their tantrums; as they learned to walk.

REMBRANDT'S HOUSE

Rembrandt and Saskia moved into Number 4, Breestraat on 1 May 1639. They were to live there for the next 20 years. Records show that Rembrandt was slow to pay for the house even by the standards of the day. When he was made insolvent in 1656 the house had to be sold to pay his creditors.

THE ZUIDERKERK

The infant mortality rate across Europe in the 17th century was well over 50 per cent. The first three babies born to Saskia and Rembrandt died when they were very young. They were buried in the local church, the Zuiderkerk, which eventually had a happier significance for them as their fourth child, Titus, was baptised there in September 1641.

RETURN OF THE DUTCH EAST INDIA FLEET

Amsterdam was the centre for north European sea-trade and the city's wealth was generated by commerce with the East. Descartes, who lived in Amsterdam, wrote in 1631 '*If there is pleasure in seeing the fruits of our orchard grow, don't you think there will be as much in seeing ships arriving bringing us in abundance all that the Indies produce and all that is rare in Europe? What other country could one choose where all the conveniences of life and all the exotic things one could desire are found so easily?*'
The contemporary view quite clearly illustrated in this passage is that the world was a fruitful 'orchard' to be cultivated by the Dutch in order that they could harvest its wealth for their benefit. Rembrandt owned a pair

of globes and could trace the voyages of the ships which were to benefit the merchants of Amsterdam and so benefit him.

RESTING PLACE

Hendrickje died on 24 July 1663 and had a simple burial in the local church, the Westerkerk. Titus died in 1668 and again was buried in the Westerkerk. On 4 October 1669, aged 63 years, Rembrandt died and was buried alongside his son and partner. We do not know what he died of, and his grave in the cemetery at the Westerkerk has never been identified.

THE BOTANICAL GARDENS AT LEIDEN UNIVERSITY

Leiden University, founded in 1575, had an excellent reputation throughout Europe for its medical, scientific and theological studies. The university was well known for its botanical garden which cultivated plants thought to be of medicinal value.

THE LIFE OF REMBRANDT

~1647~
Hendrickje Stoffels joins household as housekeeper

~1649~
Geertje and Rembrandt split up

~1652-1654~
Dutch at war with the English

~1654~
Daughter Cornelia is born to Rembrandt and Hendrickje

~1656~
Rembrandt is declared insolvent

~1658~
All Rembrandt's possessions including his house are sold to pay his creditors. Rembrandt had amassed a large collection of drawings and prints which were auctioned to raise money to pay his debts

~1660~
Titus and Hendrickje set up an art dealership and employ Rembrandt

~1663~
Hendrickje dies and is buried at the Westerkerk

~1668~
Titus dies and is buried at the Westerkerk

~1669~
Baptism of Rembrandt's grand-daughter Titia. Rembrandt dies and is buried in an unmarked grave at the Westerkerk

WHAT DO THE PAINTINGS SAY?

Rembrandt's commissioned portrait work took him from his home town of Leiden to Amsterdam, where he eventually settled. In 1632 Rembrandt painted one of the most important commissions in his career, that of *The Anatomy Lesson of Dr Tulp*. The dissection of corpses was considered illegal until shortly before Rembrandt's time, and then it was only the corpses of criminals which could be dissected. Dissections took place in lecture halls for teaching purposes. These halls were based on circular theatres with banked seats, and were called Theatres of Anatomy. In 1632 it was not uncommon for the professors and medical students to be joined by the public at large, seated on the outer benches, drawn by the macabre novelty of the occasion.

Calcoen holds in his left hand the top of the skull of Joris Fonteijn, hanged for robbery the previous day. His right hand is turned back away from his body to prevent blood from the corpse getting on his clothes.

THE ANATOMY LESSON OF DR JOAN DEYMAN, 1656

This picture was painted in 1656, some 24 years after the first anatomy picture, and it is a credit to Rembrandt's standing that the Guild of Surgeons returned to him for this commission. This too was a group portrait but much of the painting was destroyed by fire in 1723 leaving us today with only the central section.

Dr Deyman's hands can be seen performing a dissection of the brain. Deyman, Tulp's successor as Praelector (lecturer), was originally surrounded by the guild members, but only Gysbrecht Matthijsz Calcoen, Master of the Amsterdam Guild of Surgeons, survives.

Deyman performed three anatomical demonstrations, for which he was presented with six silver spoons and an amount in cash (19 stuivers) as well as income from the sale of tickets to the demonstrations, before the corpse was buried on 2 February.

The corpse is that of Adriaen Adriaansz, known as 'the Kid', who was executed for robbery. The identity of Tulp's colleagues is known because they are written on the paper held by the figure depicted behind Tulp. Number 6 on the paper is Matthijsz Calcoen whose son Gysbrecht is portrayed in Rembrandt's picture of *The Anatomy Lesson of Dr Deyman*. At the corpse's feet is propped open a book of anatomy.

THE ANATOMY LESSON OF DR NICOLAES TULP, 1632

This painting for the Amsterdam Guild of Surgeons was the first important public commission Rembrandt received in Amsterdam. It shows lecturer in anatomy Dr Nicolaes Tulp surrounded by his colleagues. He wears a broad brimmed hat which signified his high status in the Guild. Tulp lectured twice a week in the Anatomy Theatre in the upper storey of the meat market building although actual dissections were infrequent, perhaps two or three a year.

Tulp is dissecting the tendons which flex the hand. With his left hand he demonstrates the flexing action made possible by the tendons. It may be that Rembrandt wanted to make a particular point about the importance of the hand to surgeon and artist alike because normal practice would have dealt with body first and extremities last, mainly because of the bad odour.

15

THE RICH MAN FROM THE PARABLE, 1627

This has been identified as the Parable of the Rich Fool from the Book of Luke (12:13). An old man studies a coin by the light of a candle; surrounding him are tally sheets and ledgers with Hebrew script and bags of money. The story from the Bible tells of a man who becomes rich after fruitful harvests. He pulls down his barns to build bigger ones and lives off the stored riches. But '...*God said Thou fool, this night thy soul shall be required of thee, then whose shall those things be, which thou hast provided? So is he that layeth up treasure for himself, and is not rich towards God*',

Rembrandt paints the scene on the very night that the rich man's soul shall be required. In the shadows stands a clock, symbolising that his time is about to run out.

In front of him on the table are the goldsmith's scales.

WHAT DO THE PAINTINGS SAY?

T he Bible was the source of inspiration for a large number of Rembrandt's paintings. Rembrandt turned especially to the Old Testament stories, which he painted as convincing scenes from history. He may have been influenced in his subject matter by his many Jewish friends and neighbours. Rembrandt lived in an area of Leiden populated by Jews and we know he often spent time in deep discussion with these friends. These pictures were largely imaginary scenes but populated with models or figurative references to existing paintings. Painting these pictures enabled Rembrandt to create the scenes he must have imagined in his head when as a boy his mother read these Old and New Testament stories to him.

To the left and behind the figure of Jesus stand the towers of the Temple of Jerusalem.

JESUS AS A GARDENER

Rembrandt paints the moment when Mary realises that the man standing behind her is not the gardener but in fact Jesus, risen from the dead. Rembrandt makes the story recognisable by placing a gardener's hat on Jesus' head and a spade in his hand.

CHRIST AND ST. MARY MAGDALEN AT THE TOMB, 1638

This painting, which tells the story of Mary Magdalen's encounter with Jesus after the resurrection, is typical of Rembrandt's history painting. The depiction of classical history, mythology, or biblical stories was a strong tradition in art and considered for many years to be the highest form of art. The term 'history painting' does in fact mean to tell a story (the French word for story is *histoire*) and we should remember that the artist is telling a story about an historical event. In this painting Mary Magdalen has returned to the empty tomb and on seeing two angels who ask her why she is crying Mary answers *'Because they have taken away my Lord, and I know not where they have laid him'*. Rembrandt's scene attempts to capture the moment of truth for Mary Magdalen, emphasised by the light which falls on her surprised face, rather than the point in the story usually depicted by artists when Mary reaches to touch Jesus to confirm what her eyes have seen. Jesus then replies *'Touch me not'* (noli me tangere).

Rembrandt includes the jar of ointment and the cloth with which Mary Magdalen intended to anoint the body of Jesus.

SELF-PORTRAIT, c1661

Perhaps one of the best known of all Rembrandt's self-portraits, this was painted in about 1661 when he was 55. In this painting Rembrandt shows us the working artist, with palette, brushes and maulstick in hand. This is a man who is stripped of all pretension and stands resolute despite the problems that have befallen him. He was by now a widower, having suffered the loss of three children shortly after birth as well as his wife, and was bankrupt. His partner and surviving son, Titus, saved him from ruin by forming a firm of art dealers and employing Rembrandt, enabling him to continue painting.

SELF-PORTRAIT AS A YOUNG MAN, 1629

At the age of 23, Rembrandt portrays a proud and elegant young man. He has given himself a fashionable lovelock across his forehead and made his nose less bulbous than it probably was in reality by careful use of light and shadow. He had studied painting in Leiden from the age of 15 and set up as an artist sharing a studio with Jan Lievens from about 1625. By 1629 Rembrandt had begun to find a market for his pictures nearby in The Hague.

SELF-PORTRAIT, c1640

A more mature Rembrandt looks out at us in this picture despite his relative youth at only 34. The painting is clearly based upon a picture by the 16th-century Italian master Titian called *Portrait of a Young Man* (now in the National Gallery, London). It is likely that Rembrandt had come across the Titian painting while it was in the possession of the merchant Alfonso Lopez who lived in Amsterdam at the time. Interestingly Rembrandt has dressed himself not in contemporary clothes but in the earlier style of the 16th century and may have been imitating the fashion of the Italian man in Titian's portrait.

WHAT DO THE PAINTINGS SAY?

Rembrandt left us a series of self-portraits which covered all of his life as an artist. It is by this extraordinary record that we have come to know him through the stages of his life; the successful young painter; the lonely widower; the bankrupt; the old man. What comes across in all these pictures is a directness, an honesty not only to examine the true physical appearance but a lack of vanity. This is the Rembrandt who created the great portraits of men and women around him which tell us about Dutch life in the 1600s. Rembrandt's self-examination has created a precedent which many artists have followed.

SELF-PORTRAIT,
(detail) c1669

Probably the last self-portrait and certainly made in his last year of life, Rembrandt now looks every bit of his 63 years. He is now alone apart from his grand-daughter Titia. His partner Hendrickje Stoffels is dead as is his son, Titus, who died a year earlier in February 1668. When Rembrandt died on 4 October 1669 he left nothing but some clothes and his paints.

HOW WERE THEY MADE?

Painting in the age of Rembrandt was a highly skilled profession that required a good technical understanding of how to make and use paint as well as how to create an illusion on a flat plane. A great deal of investigation has gone into the methods used by Rembrandt. Paintings have been ascribed to Rembrandt and others have been judged not to be by Rembrandt as a result of these investigations. It is impossible to know with certainty whether the paintings we say today are by the master's hand include all of his works or for that matter do not include some by other artists, perhaps studio apprentices of Rembrandt. It was common practice for studio assistants to help with the painting of large canvases, the master painting the important features, but there is no evidence that Rembrandt's studio pupils did so. Some pupils did however copy Rembrandt's style closely and it is easy to see how they might be mistaken for Rembrandt's own hand after a period of several hundred years.

BENEATH THE SURFACE

Some paintings were made on oak panels, some on canvas. The surface was prepared with a white ground base. This was either a chalk mix in the case of wooden panels, or white oil paint in the case of canvas. It is likely that Rembrandt used a paint called *Hollands lootwit* to prepare the surface, a mixture of lead white and chalk (above) that was commonly available in Amsterdam. It was normal practice to tint the ground with a brown layer of paint which was then covered with further layers of transparent colour. The underpainting was known as 'dead colour'. The artist built up a complete monochrome picture filling in all the compositional features, including the light and dark tones.

CREATING COLOURS

Making colours could be a laborious process. A colour often used by Rembrandt was lead-tin yellow. In order to obtain this it was necessary to melt lead in a stone crucible, add tin at high temperature and remove the lead-tin yellow which had formed on the surface of the molten metal.

THE ARTIST IN HIS STUDIO, 1628

This is thought to be a self-portrait of the artist in his studio in Leiden in about 1629. Rembrandt holds a palette, maulstick and brushes in his hand. Behind him stands a grinding-stone on which pigments would have been ground for mixing with the oil medium prior to painting. Two clean palettes hang on the wall, ready for use.

THE COLOUR SOURCE

Rembrandt had colour pigments ground into powder before mixing them with oil and then applying the colours over the underpainting. Both charred oak (left) and charred deer antler (for bone black) were ground as a source of black pigment. Willow or vine was charred to make charcoal sticks for drawing. When the colours were ready they were applied area by area rather than across the whole picture in one go, as artists have tended to do since the 19th century. Rembrandt's paintings are famous for the experimental ways in which he applied paint, a mixture of smooth glazes (transparent layers) and impasto (thick rough textured paint) which can make some pictures look very modern.

21

Towards the back stands Jan Visscher Cornelisz, the ensign holding aloft the coat-of-arms of Amsterdam with its bands of blue and gold with embroidered lions.

At the back stands the troop jester in top hat, tentatively identified as Amsterdam wine merchant Walich Schellingwou.

It would seem that the members of the guard paid about 100 guilders each for the commission, some more some less depending on the place they had in it.

Perhaps the most mysterious figures are the two young girls who run between the soldiers, one almost completely obscured by the other. The foremost is dressed in bright yellow and has a chicken tied by its legs to her belt. One supposition is that she is a carrier to a banquet, another is that the guard is turning out for target practice and the chicken is one of the targets.

The 'powder monkey' with his powder horn hanging around his neck runs blind, sight obscured by the oversize helmet.

Rembrandt shows the three stages of musketry; the figure on the left in red loads the musket; the figure immediately behind Banning Cocq fires; the figure behind Ruytenburch blows away the used powder from the musket pan.

22

FAMOUS IMAGES

The most famous of all Rembrandt's paintings is *The Night Watch*. This group portrait painted in 1642 is of the local Amsterdam civil guard led by Captain Frans Banning Cocq and Lieutenant Willem van Ruytenburch. There was a strong tradition of these militia paintings in Amsterdam by the time Rembrandt made this one. The title is now familiar all over the world but it is misleading. It comes from the belief that the militia are being turned out at night because of the dark nature of the picture but this was in fact due to the darkening varnish and accumulation of dirt over the years. Restoration and cleaning in the 20th century revealed the painting to show a daytime scene. The original title of the painting, as so often in the case of Rembrandt, is unknown to us. The painting was commissioned as a portrait of the civic guard who were among the more important citizens of Amsterdam. The painting was to be displayed in the Great Hall of the Civic Guards, the Kloveniersdoelen. Rembrandt had lived next door to this hall for a time. What sets Rembrandt's picture apart from the traditional style is the sense of movement and action. In the more formal group portrait reality is sacrificed for the sake of equal emphasis on all portrayed.

At the centre of the painting stands Captain Frans Banning Cocq, dressed in the black of the governing class. He was not only captain of the civic guard but also Lord of the Manor of Purmerland and Ilpendam, councillor and future colonel.

Beside Cocq stands Lieutenant Willem van Ruytenburch resplendent in yellow with white and gold, boots and spurs. He was also the Lord of the Manor of Vlaerdingen.

FAMOUS IMAGES

*I*t is hard to say whether Rembrandt was a religious person. There are no records to indicate that he belonged to a particular church or sect but we do know that the religious tolerance demonstrated in Amsterdam at the time meant he would have mixed with people of different beliefs. The Jewish community in Amsterdam was largely a result of Jews escaping from religious persecution in Spain and Portugal. Rembrandt had many Jewish friends and acquaintances and perhaps it was their influence that led him to paint Old Testament themes such as Belshazzar's Feast, based on Daniel Chapter 5:

'In the same hour came forth fingers of a man's hand, and wrote over against the candlestick upon the plaister of the wall of the king's palace; and the king saw the part of the hand that wrote.

'Then the king's countenance changed, and his thoughts troubled him, so that the joints of his loins were loosed, and his knees smote one against another'.

King Belshazzar is struck with terror. His light profile against the dark background draws the viewer's eye to his face and the drama of the moment. His head-dress (turban and crown) is largely imagined because Rembrandt had no actual reference for the figures.

The woman behind Belshazzar registers open-mouthed surprise as the hand appears. The face is very like that of Saskia, Rembrandt's first wife, who probably posed for the scene.

PORTRAIT OF MENASSEH BEN ISRAEL

Menasseh was a Rabbi who lived across the street from Rembrandt. His family had fled the religious inquisitions in their home country of Portugal. Menasseh was a learned man who taught and published books as well as preaching in the local synagogue. He and Rembrandt became good friends who often passed time discussing religious subjects such as the problem of how the hand in the story of Belshazzar could have written a message which could only be deciphered by Daniel. Menasseh published a book in 1639 which explained how the letters could be written to give hidden messages by using a secret code. Rembrandt adopted this for his painting.

Rembrandt went to great lengths to ensure that the Hebrew words were authentic. The message reads 'Mene mene tekel upharsin' which translates as 'God hath numbered thy kingdom, and brought it to an end. Thou art weighed in the balances and art found wanting. Thy kingdom is divided, and given to the Medes and Persians'. The letters read vertically rather than horizontally and from right to left. This would explain why in the Old Testament story Belshazzar's men could not understand the message but Daniel, who knew the secret way of writing the Jewish letters, could read it.

BELSHAZZAR'S FEAST, 1635

The story tells of how Belshazzar, King of Babylon, laid on a feast for his wives and concubines and friends, and praised the *'…gods of gold and of silver, and of brass, of iron, of wood, and of stone'*. He served the wine in vessels which his father, Nebuchadnezzar, had looted from the Temple in Jerusalem. During the feast a mysterious hand appeared and wrote a message on the wall. Belshazzar offered a reward including a gold chain to whoever could decipher the message. Only the prophet Daniel could read the writing which foretold the loss of Belshazzar's kingdom and his imminent death. That night the city was overrun, Belshazzar was killed and the kingdom taken by Darius of the Medes.

Rembrandt's depiction of the woman on the right attempts ambitious foreshortening. The scene is reminiscent of the Italian baroque style with dramatic movement and light. Note the wine soaking into the sleeve of the woman's dress.

REMBRANDT'S PATRONS

here was a ready market for paintings in Holland in the 17th century. Artists would paint scenes and citizens of all classes would buy these paintings. Some artists however specialised in commissioned works, and prices for pictures would be calculated on the hours spent by the artist working on them. There is for example a record of the artist Adriaen van der Werff (1659-1722) charging 45 guilders per day. A painting would typically take 10 weeks to complete – thus the cost would be 3,150 guilders. It was necessary for artists who relied on commissions to entertain their patrons and socialise in the right circles. It appeared that Rembrandt would have none of this. He did not show any interest in winning influential friends and even alienated customers whose portraits he painted by insisting they sit for unacceptably long hours. Rembrandt sometimes delayed finishing paintings and on several occasions the paintings were returned by customers unhappy that they were not finished to their satisfaction.

The Suyckerbackerij on Binnen-Amstel, Rembrandt's home from 1637-1639.

Number 2-4 Jodenbreestraat, Rembrandt's home from 1639-1658. Rembrandt was forced to sell his home in the Breestraat and moved to Number 184 Rozengracht where he lived until his death in 1669.

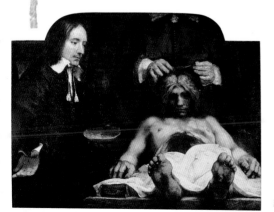

The Sint-Anthonis Weighhouse Surgeon's Guild Halls. It was in the Guild Hall rooms that Rembrandt's paintings of *The Anatomy Lesson of Dr Nicolaes Tulp* and later *The Anatomy Lesson of Dr Deyman* hung.

The Kloveniersdoelen, where *The Night Watch* hung in the Grand Hall. Rembrandt lived next door at number 20 Nieuwe Doelenstraat between 1635 and 1637, and must have seen the civic guard turn out many times.

PORTRAIT OF JAN SIX (*detail*)

At number 103 Kloveniersburgwal lived burgomaster Jan Six. Six was a friend and patron of Rembrandt, buying at least three paintings and in 1653 loaning Rembrandt 1,000 guilders. In 1654 Rembrandt painted a magnificent portrait of Six which can still be seen in Amsterdam today.

REMBRANDT'S AMSTERDAM

Van Berkenrode's map of Amsterdam shows the district where Rembrandt lived. The destination for many of his pictures could be found within a short walk of his house. Many of his commissions were for wealthy local merchants, others for civic patrons such as the civic guard and surgeon's guild. Within a short walk of Rembrandt's house stood the local Synagogue where his good friend Menasseh ben Israel preached. This map illustrates just a few of the many local places where Rembrandt's paintings hung.

SALOME WITH THE HEAD OF JOHN THE BAPTIST

Titian

The work of Titian was widely admired throughout Europe by the time of Rembrandt even though he had died only 30 years before Rembrandt's birth. Italian writer Giorgio Vasari described Titian's work in a book about his life which was translated into Dutch in 1604. Vasari describes Titian's technique for his later paintings as 'pittura di macchia' (painting with splotches). At the time this was put down to Titian's old age and failing eyesight but today we understand it to be a deliberately freer style, painting directly without preparing the canvas with drawings. This freer style has had a huge impact on the way painting has developed.

DETAIL FROM THE PORTRAIT OF JAN SIX

Critics have pointed out that Rembrandt would have been aware of the 'rough' splotchy style of Titian as opposed to the dominant 'smooth' style in Holland at the time. It is quite clear from this detail of the *Portrait of Jan Six* (see page 27), painted in 1654, that Rembrandt adopted the direct method of painting with brush strokes rapidly and freely applied to describe form and colour. For the picture to be fully appreciated it should be viewed from a certain distance, as Rembrandt himself pointed out when referring to another painting in a letter to a friend. Confirmation of this may be found in a story by writer Arnold Houbraken in 1718 relating that Rembrandt would prevent viewers in his studio getting too close to his canvases allegedly because they would be bothered by the smell of paint.

WHAT THE CRITICS SAY

Critics have been assessing the works of Rembrandt for the last 300 years and as with all artists his work has been in and out of favour with the passing of time. Today, however, all acknowledge him as one of the greatest painters in the history of art. It has sometimes been difficult for historians to recognise Rembrandt's paintings among the many works which are said to be by the master's hand. The difference between a painting acknowledged to be by Rembrandt and that of an apprentice is great if measured in financial terms. But if a painting thought to be by Rembrandt, such as the *Man with the Golden Helmet*, is then pronounced by the art historians to be by an apprentice, how does it change in our eyes? Is it a lesser picture because we know it is not a Rembrandt, is our enjoyment of it less?

PORTRAIT OF A WOMAN *(detail) Govert Flinck*

Flinck was a pupil of Rembrandt, working in his studio and painting in the style of the master. One of the reasons why it has become difficult to judge what is a 'genuine' Rembrandt and what is not after so many intervening years is that many paintings by pupils and others were painted in the exact style of Rembrandt. At the beginning of the 20th-century critics acknowledged the existence of about 1,000 paintings by Rembrandt. As successive scholars have continued to look at his paintings and applied scientific methods of dating and examination this number has gradually fallen. Doubtless as the work continues the number of 'real' Rembrandt paintings may fall still further.

THE JEWISH BRIDE

Another great artist, Vincent van Gogh, visited the Rijksmuseum in Amsterdam in 1885 and said this about Rembrandt's painting of *The Jewish Bride*: '*Do you know that I would give ten years of my life if I could sit here before this picture a fortnight, with nothing but a crust of dry bread for food*'.

STUDY FOR THE SURPRISED NYMPH, 1859-1861

Édouard Manet

This painting by Manet was inspired by Rembrandt's *Susanna and the Elders* (shown below) and *Bathsheba with King David's Letter* painted over 200 years earlier.
The subject is timeless, the interpretation different each time. Manet's model is that of his wife Suzanne Leenhoff.

THE REMBRANDT ROOM AT THE NATIONAL GALLERY, LONDON

Each year literally millions of visitors pass through the museums and galleries that contain works by Rembrandt. The National Gallery in London is a typical example, having a fine collection of Rembrandt pictures on show, but how many people really look at the paintings? Despite all the words in all the books written about Rembrandt and his art there is only one way to truly appreciate the artist: go and look at his paintings.

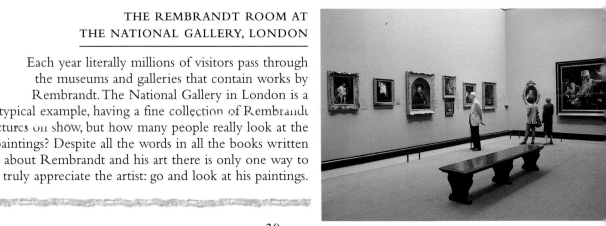

A LASTING IMPRESSION

Rembrandt has become one of the most famous names in the history of art. His influence on the work of artists who were to follow has been profound. Rembrandt fever reached a pitch in 1906 on the 300th anniversary of his birth. Some reactions were cooler. This poem mocked the public's enthusiasm for his work.

'*On the settee*
    Next to the fop with turned up nose
    The frail anaemic liberal rose
    Swoons in front of widow Bas -
    A dame of sterner stuff, alas,
    Than he or she!'

Rembrandt's obsessive analysis of himself through his series of self-portraits has to a large degree contributed to the notion of the artist as introspective examiner of the soul as well as portrayer of the world or story-teller. This view is popular today but may be discounted in 100 years' time - people cannot help but see his art in a way that is informed by the thinking of the day.

PORTRAIT OF A LADY WITH WHITE COLLAR AND CUFFS *(detail)*

Ferdinand Bol

Rembrandt was extremely influential in his own lifetime. Many artists studied at the studio of Rembrandt, learning the skills in the time-honoured way. Gerrit Dou came to Rembrandt's studio at the age of 15; Govert Flinck began at 18; Ferdinand Bol at 20.

Bol was to establish himself in Amsterdam five years later and became successful, winning a great many commissions. Bol was to be a greater success in his own lifetime than Rembrandt, becoming very wealthy by the time of his death in 1680.

GLOSSARY

Burgher - The name given to respectable citizens of the trading class. The description was most commonly used in Holland and Germany.

Flora - Rembrandt chose to paint Saskia as Flora, the Italian goddess of flowers and spring. The myth tells of a nymph named Chloris being changed into Flora by Zephyr (the warm west wind) resulting in flowers coming from Flora's breath.

Judith and Holofernes - The story of Judith and Holofernes is a favourite subject for artists. Judith was the widow from the Jewish city of Bethulia which was under siege from the Assyrian army. She tricked her way into the confidence of Holofernes, the Assryian General, then cut off his head, so causing the army to flee and saving the city.

Maulstick - A long wooden stick with a wrapping of leather or cloth over the end to make a soft pad. The padded end rests against the canvas to provide a support for the artist's hand as he paints fine details.

Noli me tangere - This translates as 'touch me not' and refers to the biblical scene which describes the moment after the Resurrection of Christ when Mary Magdalene recognises Christ and stretches out her hand to touch him. Christ says 'touch me not' and tells her to go to the disciples and tell them he is risen.

Silverpoint - A method of drawing whereby a piece of silver wire held in wood, like a pencil, is used to draw on paper coated with opaque white. The mark left by the silver wire will not smudge and is indelible.

ACKNOWLEDGEMENTS

We would like to thank: Graham Rich, Tracey Pennington, and Peter Done for their assistance.
Copyright © 2009 *ticktock* Entertainment Ltd.
First published in Great Britain by *ticktock* Media Ltd., The Old Sawmill, 103 Goods Station Road, Tunbridge Wells, Kent, TN1 2DP

A CIP catalogue record for this book is available from the British Library.
ISBN 978 1 84898 042 6
Printed in China.
9 8 7 6 5 4 3 2 1

Acknowledgements: Picture Credits t=top, b=bottom, c=centre, l=left, r=right, OFC=outside front cover, IFC=inside front cover, IBC=inside back cover, OBC=outside back cover.

Akademie der Bildenden Kuenste, Vienna. Photo © AKG London/Erich Lessing; 5cl. Photo © AKG London; 3t, 6/7ct. Photo credit: Bridgeman Art Library, London; 2bl. By permission of The British Library (1790b 21 Sheet 3); 26/27c. Copyright © British Museum; 12/13c. Christie's Images/Bridgeman Art Library, London; 28tr. Courtauld Gallery, London/Bridgeman Art Library, London; 8c. Dahlem Staatliche Gemaldegalerie, Berlin/Bridgeman Art Library, London; 10bl & 30cr. Fitzwilliam Museum, University of Cambridge/Bridgeman Art Library, London; 5t. Galleria degli Uffizi, Florence. Photo © AKG London; 7bl. Kenwood House, London/Bridgeman Art Library, London; 18tl. Mary Evans Picture Library; 3bl, 3br. Mauritshuis, The Hague. Photo © AKG London; 7br. Mauritshuis, The Hague. Photo © AKG London/Erich Lessing; 15tl & 26br. Mauritshuis, The Hague/Bridgeman Art Library, London; OBC & 18cr, OFCl & 19br. Musee du Louvre, Paris. Photo © AKG London; 6tl. Musee du Louvre, Paris. Photo © AKG London/Erich Lessing; 6cr, 11t. Museo del Prado, Madrid. Photo © AKG London/Erich Lessing; 6cl. Nasjonalgalleriet, Oslo/Giraudon/Bridgeman Art Library, London; 30cl. Reproduced by courtesy of the Trustees, The National Gallery, London; 4bl & 18bl, 30br. National Gallery, London/Bridgeman Art Library, London; OFCr & 25. National Maritime Museum, London; 13tl. Private Collection, Amsterdam/Bridgeman Art Library, London; 27br. Rafael Valls Gallery, London/Bridgeman Art Library, London; 31r. Rijksmuseum, Amsterdam. Photo © AKG London; OBC & IFC/1 & 22/23 & 27tr, 14bl & 26bl, 30tr. The Royal Collection © Her Majesty Queen Elizabeth II; 17. © Sidney Moulds/Garden Picture Library; 4br. SMPK, Gemaeldegalerie, Berlin. Photo © AKG London; 8br, OBC & 16t. Staatliches Kunstmuseum, Bucharest. Photo © AKG London; 29r. Victoria & Albert Museum, London/Bridgeman Art Library, London; 2tl. Wallace Collection, London/Bridgeman Art Library, London; 9br. Zoë Oliver Sherman Collection. Given in memory of Lillie Oliver Poor. Courtesy of Museum of Fine Arts, Boston; 21t.

Every effort has been made to trace the copyright holders and we apologise in advance for any unintentional omissions. We would be pleased to insert the appropriate acknowledgement in any subsequent edition of this publication.

Curriculum Visions

Children in the Second World War

Children in a trench dug across a park and used as a simple bomb shelter.

Dr Brian Knapp

> "This morning the British Ambassador in Berlin handed the German government a final note stating that unless we heard from them by 11 o'clock, that they were prepared at once to withdraw their troops from Poland, a state of war would exist between us. I have to tell you now that no such undertaking has been received and that consequently this country is at war with Germany."
>
> Neville Chamberlain,
> Prime Minister, 3 September 1939

▲ VE-Day, when huge numbers of people gathered outside Buckingham Palace, London.

Curriculum Visions

There's much more on-line including videos

You will find multimedia resources covering the Second World War and many more history, science, geography, religion and spelling subjects in the Professional Zone at:

www.CurriculumVisions.com

A CVP Book
Copyright Earthscape © 2007

First reprint 2007

The right of Brian Knapp to be identified as the author of this work has been asserted by him in accordance with the Copyright, Designs and Patents Act 1988.

Author
Brian Knapp, BSc, PhD

Senior Designer
Adele Humphries, BA, PGCE

Editors
Jan Smith (former Deputy Head of Wellfield School, Burnley, Lancashire) and Gillian Gatehouse

Designed and produced by
EARTHSCAPE

Printed in China by
WKT Company Ltd

Children in the Second World War – *Curriculum Visions*
A CIP record for this book is available from the British Library

Paperback ISBN 978 1 86214 228 2
Hardback ISBN 978 1 86214 229 9

Illustrations
David Woodroffe

Picture credits
All photographs are from the Earthscape Picture Library except the following: (c=centre t=top b=bottom l=left r=right)
Corbis pages 6t, 10–11, 16, 20, 21, 22b, 23, 24–25, 38, 42, 43; *Glamorgan Archives* pages 18–19; *A friend of the Dilke Memorial Hospital* pages 30–31; *The Granger Collection, New York* pages 17, 27; *The Illustrated London News* pages 6bl, 14–15, 29; *Imperial War Museum* pages 18tl, 32, 36–37, 37, 40–41; *Library of Congress* cover and pages 1, 2, 13br, 44c, 46–47; *The National Archives* pages 22t, 28, 45; *ShutterStock* pages 5, 12–13 (Spitfire), 12c, 39. The publishers have made their best endeavours to contact all copyright holders for material published in this book.

This product is manufactured from sustainable managed forests. For every tree cut down at least one more is planted.

Contents

Note: in this book the term 'Britain' is used as a shorthand, meaning "The United Kingdom of Great Britain and Northern Ireland".

Words in **BOLD CAPITALS** are further explained in the glossary on pages 46 and 47.

▲ A cross remembering those who fell during the world wars.

What was the Second World War?

The Second World War affected many countries in the world. A group of countries – Germany, Italy and Japan – fought the allied countries (ALLIES) of Britain, its Commonwealth partners and the USA.

War – it's one of the most terrifying words in any language, yet it has happened in every century since records began. Many of these wars happened a long time ago and may not seem real to us.

However, the Second World War (World War II) is different (picture ①). Your grandparents may have been alive during or just after this war and can still tell you of their memories.

Britain and allies
Germany and allies
Controlled by Germany and allies
Neutral

▼ ① Areas controlled by the warring nations in the early days of the war.

▲ ② **Remembrance Day (11 November) is a special day when we remember men and women killed during the two World Wars and other conflicts.**

If you look around, you may think there are few signs of the Second World War. There are MEMORIALS, of course (picture ② and pages 3, 8 and 9). But is there anything else? In fact, many of the huge changes that have happened to Britain in recent years were brought about by that war.

In this book you will find out what it was like to be in the war, and you will find hints as to why life after the war has never been the same.

Why did the war start?

No wars start for simple reasons. Usually they start because of things that had been happening for a long time.

Some of the causes of World War II can be found in World War I, that ended 25 years earlier. At the end of that war, in 1918, Germany signed a peace treaty which the German people thought was very unfair.

For years after World War I, the Germans had little to eat, few jobs and they felt they had lost their pride and honour. This was a dangerous time because they could easily be persuaded by unscrupulous people that there was honour, glory and a better life ahead. After all, what could be worse?

► ① A class being taught about Hitler in 1939.

▼ ② Adolf Hitler was one of the worst dictators the world has ever known. Yet he was able to portray himself to Germans as a kindly father figure, as this picture shows.

The Nazi party

This was how a small, extreme party was able to come to power. It was called the National Socialist Party, which came to be known as the **NAZI** Party. Its ruthless leader was Adolf Hitler (pictures ① and ②).

Hitler was a very powerful speaker and his speeches persuaded people to believe in him as their leader. Away from the public eye he was ruthless and had no problem in killing people to take control of the Nazi Party.

Second World War timeline

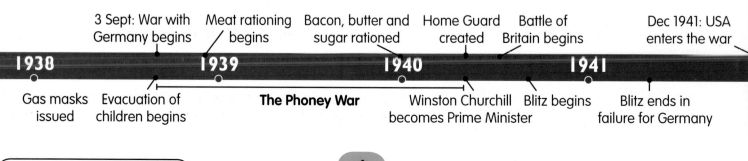

| 1938 | 1939 | 1940 | 1941 |

3 Sept: War with Germany begins

Meat rationing begins

Bacon, butter and sugar rationed

Home Guard created

Battle of Britain begins

Dec 1941: USA enters the war

Gas masks issued

Evacuation of children begins

The Phoney War

Winston Churchill becomes Prime Minister

Blitz begins

Blitz ends in failure for Germany

By 1933, public charm and private treachery had moved him into the most powerful position in Germany. Soon he became the military **DICTATOR** of the country.

People followed him because his policies started to provide more jobs and made people better off. He rebuilt the German army and this gave the Germans pride.

He then told people that they needed more living space and they simply had no alternative but to take it, just as peoples had done in the past. This meant invading Germany's neighbours. As a result, war came ever closer.

The Nazis' dark side

The Nazis were very skilled at getting their message across. This is called **PROPAGANDA** (and in modern times, 'spin'). What they said was not always the truth.

The dark side of the Nazis was truly horrible, with Jews, gypsies and many other people being rounded up and put into **CONCENTRATION CAMPS** and killed. But somehow the German people did not wake up to this.

Germany over-runs Europe

Hitler was a bold planner. He pushed and pushed against the rules of the peace treaty and the other European countries did nothing to stop him.

In Britain, the Prime Minister, Neville Chamberlain, was a very good man, but for the times he was too weak. As a result, Adolf Hitler was able to re-arm and take over other countries, while Britain – then one of the most powerful countries in the world – stood by. At the same time the United States did not want to be involved in another war and so they stood idly by, too.

Soon, Germany made agreements with other bad governments, such as Italy, Russia and Japan.

War with Britain begins

Britain had agreed to protect Poland. So when Germany invaded Poland on 3 September 1939, Neville Chamberlain was forced to declare war on Germany. Because Germany was allied with countries such as Italy and Japan, and because Britain had colonies across the world, this meant that this war was a World War.

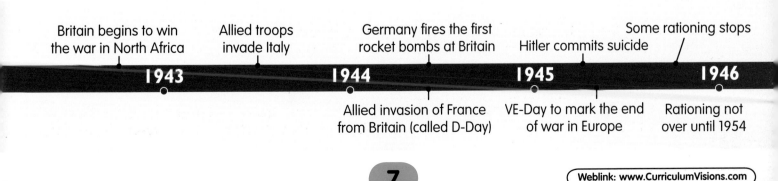

Britain begins to win the war in North Africa

Allied troops invade Italy

Germany fires the first rocket bombs at Britain

Hitler commits suicide

Some rationing stops

1943 | **1944** | **1945** | **1946**

Allied invasion of France from Britain (called D-Day)

VE-Day to mark the end of war in Europe

Rationing not over until 1954

Weblink: www.CurriculumVisions.com

Why we have memorials

We have memorials to remind us of the sacrifice many people made in every corner of the country, and how tragic war can be.

World War II lasted six long years – from 1939 to 1945. It affected everyone in Britain, but also in the nations connected to Britain. Many of the Commonwealth countries (such as Singapore and Malaya) were overrun by the Japanese and many others countries (such as Australia, Canada, India and New Zealand) willingly sent troops to help make the world a better and safer place.

Memorials

Wherever you go in the Commonwealth you will find war **MEMORIALS** (pictures ① and ②). In Britain there is one in every parish and borough. If you look at them you will see the names of people who went to fight in the war and who never came back because they were killed in action.

▼ ① These are names on a memorial. Read your local memorials and try to find out something about at least one of the people who used to live near to you.

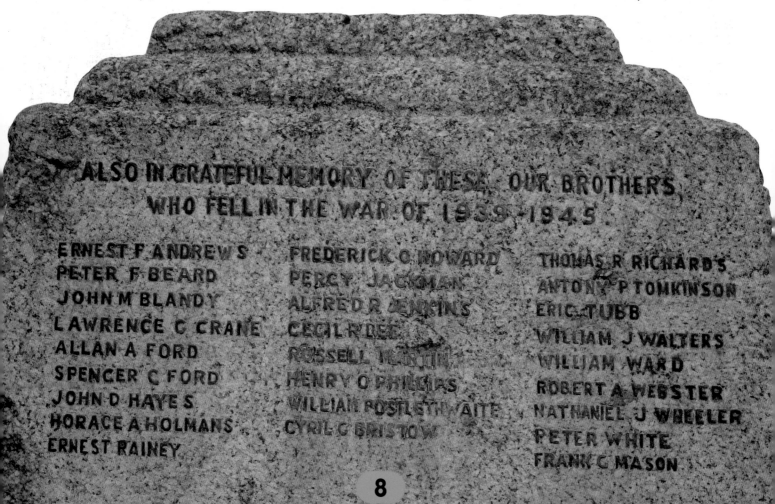

ALSO IN GRATEFUL MEMORY OF THESE OUR BROTHERS
WHO FELL IN THE WAR OF 1939-1945

ERNEST F ANDREWS
PETER F BEARD
JOHN M BLANDY
LAWRENCE C CRANE
ALLAN A FORD
SPENCER C FORD
JOHN D HAYES
HORACE A HOLMANS
ERNEST RAINEY

FREDERICK C HOWARD
PERCY JACKMAN
ALFRED R JENKINS
CECIL R BEE
RUSSELL MARTIN
HENRY O PHILLIPS
WILLIAM POSTLETHWAITE
CYRIL G BRISTOW

THOMAS R RICHARDS
ANTONY P TOMKINSON
ERIC TUBB
WILLIAM J WALTERS
WILLIAM WARD
ROBERT A WEBSTER
NATHANIEL J WHEELER
PETER WHITE
FRANK C MASON

▲ ② Many war memorials are in churchyards. The British national war memorial (the cenotaph) is in Whitehall near the Houses of Parliament.

Lost relatives

These people were someone's sons or brothers. But above all, many were fathers. A child who lived in the parish or borough may never again see their father, and would grow up after the war with a small corner of their world forever sad.

So the war affected children as well as adults.

Each year the nation remembers the people who died in the war (and those of other wars). Even though World War II ended over 60 years ago, the events leading up to the war, and the war itself, must never be forgotten, so that dreadful events like this should never be allowed to happen again.

The Battle of Britain

Because Britain is an island, the German army could not invade easily. So they began a bombing campaign.

The Germans had thought up a new kind of war. They used tanks (panzers) and bomb-carrying planes (picture ①).

This new fast attack was meant to end any war quickly. In fact, the Germans planned to conquer many parts of Europe in just a few weeks. This new kind of fast war was called Blitzkrieg in German (in English it is 'lightning war').

The German Blitzkrieg plan worked well. In a year Belgium, France, the Netherlands, Denmark and Norway were all defeated. This left Britain to stand alone against the might of Hitler's Germany.

Why Britain was special

To conquer Britain, you have to invade by sea. Britain had the world's most powerful navy, far bigger than Germany's. But most important of all, Britain also had an airforce.

◄ ① A rally in a German stadium is overflown by part of the huge German airforce. The flags show the Nazi Party swastika.

If the Germans tried to send over soldiers in ships, they could easily be destroyed by British aircraft.

So the Germans realised they needed to destroy the British air force before they could invade.

So, for Britain, the first stage of the Blitzkrieg attack was to bomb British airfields.

German air power

The Germans had a vast fleet of fighter and bomber aircraft. The British had not kept up.

11

The British had brilliant engineers who eventually made planes better than the Germans – the Spitfire (picture ②) and the Hurricane are still remembered across the world.

But it took time before the British government started to re-arm. By the start of war, the air force only had a quarter of the planes that the Germans had (640 compared to 2,500).

▼ ② The famous British Spitfire fighter plane.

The Blitzkrieg

In July 1940 bombing began with attacks on British airfields, aircraft factories and **RADAR** stations. Hitler wanted to destroy the Royal Air Force (RAF) while it was on the ground.

▼▶ ③ Just in case the Germans invaded, the British government set up many defensive gunsites. Because of their shape – low and round – they became nicknamed 'pillboxes'. Each had a gun trained on the most likely route the Germans would use.

Many pillboxes still survive in the countryside and you can visit them.

▶ ④ Germans made up this picture from two pictures, one of a plane, the other of London docks. It was never a real picture. This is an example of Nazi propaganda. They wanted their own people to see that Germany had control of the skies. In reality it did not.

The RAF commanders sent up **FIGHTER PLANES** to attack. With skill and determination they were able to shoot down large numbers of German planes (picture ④). This time was known as the Battle of Britain and the British fighters won (picture ⑤).

It was after this that the new Prime Minister, Winston Churchill, (picture ⑥) made his famous speech in which he declared:

"Never in the field of human conflict was so much owed by so many to so few."

It was nothing short of the truth.

▶ ⑤ A poster celebrating Britain's achievements in the Battle of Britain.

▶ ⑥ Winston Churchill, the Prime Minister of Britain during the war. He was 65 when the war began, but he worked tirelessly year after year.

13

The Blitz begins

The Blitz was a time when German planes bombed British cities in an effort to make the British people surrender.

Hitler did not know the strength and reserves of the RAF. In fact, the RAF were just on the edge of being defeated because they were so outnumbered. But, as he did not know this, Hitler thought that he had to find another way of defeating Britain.

As it happened, a chance event was to trigger what Hitler did next. On 24 August 1940 a lost German bomber crew accidentally bombed London instead of the airfields it had been given as a target. Prime Minister, Winston Churchill, thought the Germans had meant to attack London, so he told the RAF to bomb Berlin, the capital of Germany.

Hitler was shocked by the attack on his homeland. In a furious speech he said:

> "If they send over a hundred bombers to bomb our cities, then we shall send a thousand planes to bomb theirs. And if they think that they can destroy our cities, then we shall wipe theirs from the face of the Earth."

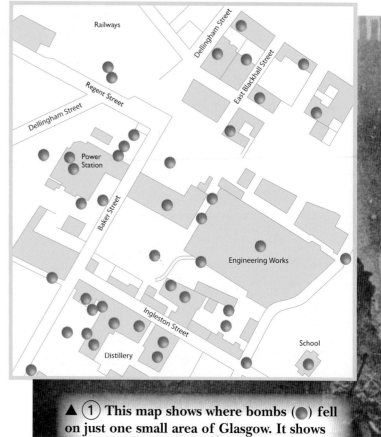

▲ ① **This map shows where bombs (●) fell on just one small area of Glasgow. It shows you how much effect bombing had.**

In a rage, Hitler ordered the German air force (the Luftwaffe) to stop attacking airfields and to attack ports and cities instead. He thought that bombing the people would make them want to ask for peace.

In fact, it had just the opposite effect. It also gave precious time for the RAF to recover and, in the long run, beat the Germans back from British skies. But that would take many months.

▼ ② This was the centre of Coventry after the night raid of 14 November 1940. The ancient cathedral and much of the city centre were destroyed.

The Blitz

The bombing of cities was the start of the time called the Blitz (the word Blitz is a shortened version of Blitzkrieg, see page 10).

The Blitz affected nearly all major cities. From early September 1940 London was attacked on 57 nights in a row and over a million bombs were dropped.

Many other important industrial cities also suffered. The whole centre of Coventry was destroyed on one fateful night (picture ②). Glasgow suffered the worst because it was so important as a centre for making ships and weapons (picture ①).

Bombing was inaccurate, so even if the targets were meant to be docks, factories and railway lines, many bombs fell on nearby houses, shelters and hospitals. As a result, over 41,000 civilians were killed during the Blitz.

Tracking the bombers

In those days, planes flew at less than 200 miles an hour (300 km/hr). It is about 70 miles (110 km) from the south coast to London, so planes coming from Germany on bombing runs would take half an hour to reach the city.

A special wireless detecting system called **RADAR** could pick them up as they started across the Channel. Those keeping watch at the coast could also telephone ahead to give **AIR-RAID WARDENS** some warning of an **AIR RAID** and tell them how many planes were involved.

In each city, a system of air-raid sirens was set up to warn people of the raid and give them time to take cover. At the same time the anti-aircraft (known as **ACK-ACK**) gun crews were told to get ready to fire on the planes as they passed overhead.

Huge barrage balloons were flown above each city (picture ③). The thick steel tethering wires made flying difficult because if a plane flew into one, the wire could cut a wing off.

Seeing an air raid

Imagine seeing the first ever wave of bombers arriving over London at about four o'clock in the afternoon of 7 September 1940. It must have been a very frightening sight.

In the sky you would have seen 340 bombers protected by 600 fighters. Their target was the docks of London and their purpose was to drop hundreds of fire bombs (see page 18) and set the docks ablaze.

There were so many planes lining up to bomb London that it took them two hours to drop their bombs.

▼ ③ Barrage balloons being raised before the start of an air raid.

Blackout

Britain depends on its docks, its shipyards and the railways and roads that carry goods from the docks to where they are needed. This is why the Germans tried to bomb port cities such as Bristol, Glasgow, Liverpool, London and Plymouth.

It is easy to pick out cities at night by their lights. It is almost like having a map to aim with.

The only answer was to have a blackout, meaning that no-one was allowed to have a light showing at night. Heavy curtains or shutters had to be placed at windows (picture ④), car headlights were fitted with special hoods so they only shone downwards, and all street lights and shop lights were turned out. Cities were therefore totally black at night.

To make sure people obeyed this instruction, blackout wardens patrolled the streets.

▲ ④ Shutters being put up on a shop window just before the blackout.

The raid continues by night

This was not the end. The first bombs caused fires and as the fires raged they made beacons of light for the night bombers. They arrived about 8 o'clock in the evening. Their raid lasted even longer – it was not until 4.30 in the morning that the last bombs were dropped and the all-clear siren was sounded.

This first day was just the beginning of one of the most horrific periods of the war for the people of Britain's cities. The Blitz lasted for nine months. During this time there was hardly a night when the air-raid sirens did not wail or that the whine of bombs and their explosions could not be heard over one of Britain's cities.

By mid-October (just a month after the start of the Blitz) there were 250,000 people homeless in London alone due to the Blitz. This meant that there was a serious problem in finding shelter for all of them.

The last raid

On 10 May 1941 a 550 bomber raid dropped more than 700 tonnes of bombs and thousands of incendiaries (fire bombs). This was probably the worst raid of the Blitz with nearly 1,500 men, women and children killed in one day. But it was also the last of the mass raids. Hitler had turned his attention towards Russia. The bombing of British cities had been a failure.

What bombs did

Bombs were the main way that Germans attacked Britain.

▼ ① A 'doodlebug' (V1 rocket).

Bombs are metal tubes packed with explosives. They are made so that one end is heavier than the other. When they are dropped from aircraft (picture ①), they fall heavy-end down so that a firing device in the nose, called a detonator, will hit the ground and set off the explosive in the bomb.

Blast bombs

There are two kinds of bomb. The most common kind is called a blast bomb. The explosive breaks up the metal case and pieces of metal – called shrapnel – are thrown in every direction. The explosive also sends out shock waves that destroy buildings (picture ②). In World War II the bombs were generally only powerful enough to knock down one house at a time.

Bombs were dropped from planes in groups, known as 'sticks'. The bombs fell in a line, each separated by a few hundred metres. The result was a trail of damage from each plane.

▲ ② Bombing destroyed some buildings completely, but it also caused damage over a wider area. Look, for example, how many houses have been destroyed in this picture (Swansea) and the burned out roof of the church.

▶ ③ Once the raid was over, people went back to their houses to see what was left, and, if their house had been destroyed, to collect anything that was left.

▼ ④ Night-time bombing with incendiary bombs left a trail of burning buildings that were like beacons for the aircraft still waiting to drop their bombs.

Fire bombs

Fire (incendiary) bombs were often the most damaging. They were packed with a mixture of explosive and chemicals that caught fire as the bomb exploded. Burning explosive was scattered over a wide area, setting buildings alight (pictures ③ and ④).

Once a fire had started it was difficult to put it out during an air raid because water pipes were often damaged. Firefighters in wartime cities were among the most heroic of the cities' people (picture ⑤).

▼ ⑤ **People were not demoralised by the bombing. If the shop was bombed out, people continued to sell their goods from a barrow in the road.**

Finding shelter

Some people used underground railway stations. Others built shelters in their gardens. Some people did not bother with protection at all.

What could people do to protect themselves from the bombs? They could hope that the RAF fighters would attack the bombers before they arrived overhead; they could give early warnings using sirens, and defend with ack-ack guns; they could dig bombproof shelters; and, most dramatically of all, they could evacuate people from cities.

LOOK before you sleep

ALL WINDOWS AND INNER DOORS OPEN?

WATER IN BUCKETS?

WATER WATER

SAND SAND

SAND IN BUCKETS?

GAS MASK, CLOTHES AND TORCH HANDY?

◀ (1) This poster told people how to be prepared for a nearby bomb hit.

GOOD NIGHT!

▶ (2) Many children were not evacuated and they stayed with their parents. When the bombs came they went to shelters, or they went down to the cellar of their house. Here is a (working CLASS) grandmother and children in a cellar. Look carefully at their clothes, how they are washing themselves and what is in the background.

▶ ③ An Anderson shelter.

In the first years of the Blitz, 150,000 Anderson shelters were provided by the government. They were made of corrugated iron.

Many people did not want to leave their homes, and even owners of Anderson shelters often preferred to shelter in a cupboard under the stairs in winter.

The Morrison shelter was an iron cage that doubled as a table. It was designed to protect the family as their house collapsed around them. The theory was that they would crawl out from the rubble unhurt. However, if they were trapped and the house was on fire, it is unlikely they could get out.

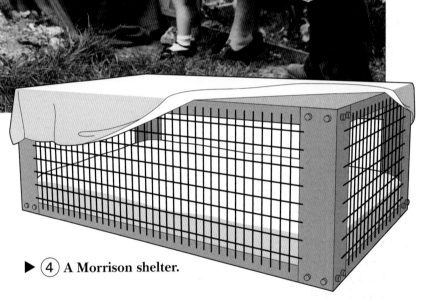

▶ ④ A Morrison shelter.

Shelters

Making bombproof shelters was difficult. To be truly bomb-proof, the shelter has to be a deep 'cave' with a reinforced concrete roof. So few were ever built. But protection could be simple. Trenches were dug in parks (away from where buildings might collapse or fires take hold) and bricked over. They gave protection from shrapnel and were safe unless there was a direct hit on the trench.

Even so, many people decided to take their chances at home (pictures ① and ②). Those with deep cellars could use those. Those with gardens were encouraged to build their own shelters, or they could even build a shelter in their living room. Each type of shelter was named after its designer – the Anderson (picture ③) and the Morrison shelters (picture ④).

For those who wanted to escape the cities, special trains were run to places in the countryside. For example, trains ran from London every night to Kent where people would sleep in caves. But these could only hold a few people.

Shelters were also needed for important factories. As well as being used as a bomb shelter (picture ⑤), some parts of the London Underground were used as factories. They were closed off from trains and the tracks concreted over. Plessey's of Ilford, for example, which supplied the RAF with aircraft parts, became a tubular factory almost 5 miles (8 km) long, employing 2,000 workers.

▼ ⑤ As German planes flew overhead, dropping their sticks of bombs, some Londoners chose to go down into the Underground system. Some slept there all night. Many, however, found them noisy and smelly and preferred to take their chances at home.

In November 1940:
- 4% were sheltering in the Underground system.
- 9% in public shelters.
- 27% in domestic shelters, such as Anderson and/or Morrison shelters. Yet 60% of Londoners still preferred to stay in their own homes, sheltering mostly in cellars, underneath stairs, or even in cupboards.

Gas masks

In World War I many soldiers had been killed and injured by poison gas released over the battlefields. As World War II approached there was real fear that poison gas might be dropped from bombs. As a result, in 1938, the government decided that everyone should be issued with a gas mask (picture ⑥) and that they must carry it at all times.

Gas masks came in many shapes and sizes. There were 'Mickey Mouse' gas masks to help younger children think they were fun. Many children discovered the design meant that it accidentally produced a 'raspberry' noise, every time they breathed through it!

Civil Defence workers had a gas mask in green. Ordinary adult gas masks were black. They were a simple rubber mask, with a plastic visor and webbing to hold it on to the head. Gas masks were even made for horses and dogs!

◄ ⑥ A 'tin' (plated steel) helmet and gas mask were issued to wardens who had to be out during an air raid.

Why were children evacuated?

People worried that many children would be killed if they stayed near the docks. So plans were made to move them to the safety of the countryside.

The government believed that there might be millions of deaths from bombing, and so in the first few days of September 1939 they planned to move a million children and their teachers (who became their guardians) from places near docks and railways where they might get bombed, to the safety of towns and villages in the countryside. This movement was called evacuation and it was known as 'Operation Pied Piper'.

It did not involve children who lived in the outer parts of cities (the suburbs) where bombs rarely fell.

Many children were not told exactly what was going to happen. Quite often they were simply told they were going on holiday with their school for a few days (picture ①).

▼ ① Young children were lined up and labels put on them, saying who they were and where they were going. They became human parcels.

▲ ②　Children were escorted in long 'crocodiles' to waiting buses.

Billeting

It was a huge problem trying to find new homes for such enormous numbers of children and then getting them from their own homes to their new destination.

A count was made of all of the spare rooms in every house in countryside villages. These were to be used as homes (**BILLETS**) for the evacuees. The process was compulsory: if you had spare rooms, you got evacuees, and you had no idea who they were and where they were coming from. It was all in the hands of a local official called a billeting officer.

Packed off like parcels

Smaller children could not understand what they were doing and there was a danger that they might get lost.

So each was treated just like a piece of luggage. Each child carried a gas mask in a box, some food and a change of clothing. They wore three labels saying who they were, where they had come from and where they were going to. Then they were told "Don't suck or eat your labels!".

Crocodiles

From the school they walked in 'crocodiles' or went in coaches with their teachers to the railway station (picture ②). Here they found themselves among tens of thousands of other children. Some thought it was all noisy and confusing, while others thought it was an exciting adventure.

When the children arrived at their destination there were often not enough spaces for them and so some

27

local people had to take more children than they were expecting (picture ④). In many cases billeting officers lined the children up in a village and asked local people to take their pick. Many children heard "I'll take that one," and then found themselves whisked off – to the unknown.

A member of the family?

In the best billets, the new arrivals were treated like a member of the family, very often moving into homes much wealthier than they had been used to. In the worst, children were mistreated by families who didn't want them and didn't care about them.

Some were children newly arrived in England. These were mainly Jewish children who had just escaped from Germany or other European countries and now they had to be evacuated again away from their parents.

Freda Skrzypee, aged nine, who arrived with her parents and brother from Danzig on Sunday was among them. She spoke no English, but had a companion in Ruth Rosenzweig, a Jewish refugee from Berlin. "The Germans have taken away our nationality," she said, "But I am happy here." (*Daily Mirror*, 1939)

Evacuation overseas

The government also arranged for children to be sent to the USA,

Reasons to evacuate

You might get killed by bombs.
Your house might get bombed and then you would have nowhere to live.
Your city school might be closed and you would have nowhere to learn.
You would go to the countryside where you could learn in a school as normal.

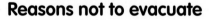

▶ ③ A poster issued after evacuation warning mothers not to bring their children back from the countryside.

Reasons not to evacuate

You might end up with a family you didn't like or who didn't like you.
You might get separated from your friends.
You would be separated from your mother.
The chances of being killed by a bomb were not as great as some people feared.
You would not be able to take much with you.

Canada and Australia. In the first few months over 210,000 were registered with the scheme. However, one of the evacuation ships was sunk by a German **TORPEDO** and 73 children were killed, so the overseas evacuation stopped.

Did evacuation work?

When war was first declared, the evacuation plan was immediately put into effect. It was voluntary and about a sixth of all those who could leave did not want to go. Then for many months there were no bombing raids. This was a time called 'The Phoney War' and so some parents thought it would be safe for their children to come back home.

Many children were also homesick. By January 1940 nearly half of all evacuated schoolchildren had returned home (picture ③). It was then that the bombing began. In the long run, it was a lot of effort and it is doubtful if it saved many lives.

What was it like for billeting families?

Remember that the children evacuated were mostly from inner city areas near docks and factories. Most were from very poor families whose contact with the world beyond their own small area was almost non-existent. There wasn't the TV to watch as there is today and few people from these areas could afford a radio. Many had hygiene standards that would shock us today.

So if it was strange for the evacuated children to go out into the countryside, when many had never seen the countryside before in their lives, it was equally strange for those watching the children arrive.

Many country people were shocked to find that half of the children coming to them were dirty, and had fleas or head lice. At that time many houses in the poorest inner city areas still did not have toilets and children were used to going to the toilet wherever they felt like it – including public places.

▲ ④ Evacuated children lining up to have their bath in front of the kitchen stove (called a range).

The Home Guard

With most of the ABLE-BODIED men away in the forces, the British government had to think of ways to protect the country in case of attack. This was how the Home Guard came about.

The government had to find some way of defending Britain when most of the forces were fighting overseas. The answer was to make a force out of those who were in essential jobs, the elderly and those a bit too young to join the forces. This was soon known as the Home Guard (picture ①).

No weapons

By the end of June 1940, there were nearly 1.5 million volunteers, but to begin with they didn't even have uniforms, just an armband that said 'LDV' (Local Defence Volunteers). They had almost no weapons, for the weapons were going to the regular troops. So they made up for this by training to observe and report any enemy movements.

To counter the threat of an airborne or coastal attack, the Home Guard manned observation posts. Home guards spent every night watching the skies and the sea, often armed with no more than a cup of tea and a pitchfork.

▼ ① A Home Guard recruitment poster telling people what a vital task they would perform.

ARE **YOU** PREPARED FOR THIS ? IF NOT, THEN JOIN YOUR LOCAL HOME GUARD

Patrols were also carried out on foot, by bicycle, even on horseback. It was not until 1943 that the Home Guard became a well equipped and trained force (picture ②).

The Home Guard were formally disbanded on 3 December 1944, six months after the invasion of Europe had begun.

▲ ③ Home Guard lapel badge.

▼ ② Home Guard practice. Note the arms have been removed from the signpost in the centre of the picture. This was done all over the country to make it more difficult for an invading enemy to know where they were.

31

▲ ① Setting off depth charges (underwater bombs) over an area where a German submarine had been detected.

Why food became scarce

Britain cannot grow enough food to feed its people, so when war broke out and ships could not reach Britain easily, food had to be rationed.

Britain is a small country with many people. It cannot grow enough food from its own land and must get the extra food needed from overseas.

By the start of World War II, Britain was importing large amounts of wheat from the United States of America and Canada.

Other foods that were imported included cheese and butter (from Australia and New Zealand) tea (from India), coffee (from Brazil), sugar (from the West Indies) and many kinds of fruit.

Food was not the only thing that had to come from overseas. Some of these vital items were petrol (from the Middle East), wood and rubber (for car tyres, from Malaya).

The Battle of the Atlantic

One of the ways the Germans believed they could beat the British was to stop these vital supplies from arriving in Britain.

As a result they sent out their battleships and submarine fleet (U-boats) to hunt down and destroy the ships carrying supplies to Britain across the Atlantic.

The Prime Minister, Winston Churchill, wrote,

> "… *the only thing that ever really frightened me during the war was the U-boat (Unterseeboot) peril.*"

The Royal Navy organised the **MERCHANT SHIPS** into groups, called convoys, which they tried to protect with destroyers, cruisers and other naval vessels.

The struggle between the German and British navies was called the Battle of the Atlantic. It was the longest battle of World War II, lasting from 1939 to 1945.

In the early years the U-boats nearly won the battle and more ships were sunk than could be built to replace them. In total, 2,500 ships were sunk. Then the navy got detecting systems called **SONAR** and **RADAR**, making it easier to find the enemy underwater (picture ①). Aircraft were designed with a longer range, so they could also help to protect the convoys by spotting the U-boats and even bombing them.

Rationing

As there were limited supplies of food and other essentials, the government decided that the fairest thing was to give rich and poor the same amount. They did this by rationing food and other items.

The ships that crossed the Atlantic during the war could only carry the most essential foods, such as flour for bread and sugar for preserving fruits. Most foods that had once been imported soon vanished completely from the grocer's shelves. There were, for example, few oranges and no bananas at all for six years. Tea and coffee were thought of as essential foods. Milk was concentrated and put in cans, so was beef – it became corned beef, while concentrated pork became spam.

Rationing

Because there was less food coming in to the country the government decided to give everyone the same fair share of the scarce resources – whether they were rich or poor. The scheme was called RATIONING, and food that was rationed was only available through coupons in a specially issued ration book (picture ①).

▲ ① **Ration coupons for sugar, butter and margarine, and ham and bacon.**

Radio broadcasts told people of changes to the rations.

Everyone took part in rationing – even the Royal Family.

Ration books had to be renewed and new ones issued every Summer.

Everyone had to register with their local shop and the shopkeeper was then given enough food for their registered customers by the Ministry of Food.

If the shop where people were registered happened to be bombed they had to register with another shop in order to use their ration book and buy their goods.

WHAT DID PEOPLE EAT DURING THE WAR?

DATES ITEMS ARE RATIONED

29 September 1939	8 January 1940	March 1941	February 1942	21 July 1946
National Register set up and Identity Cards issued.	**Rationing begins** Butter: 4oz* Sugar: 12oz Bacon: 4oz	Jam: 8oz Cheese: 2oz	Soap: 1 small tablet (per month)	Bread: 9oz (per day) (part of which could be taken as flour or cakes)

NATIONAL REGISTRATION IDENTITY CARD

NATIONAL BUTTER

SUGAR

March 1940	June 1941	June 1942
Meat: 1s. 10d (9p)	Eggs: 1 fresh egg Meat: 1s (5p)	American dried egg powder on sale.

July 1940

No more bananas or fruit (except a few oranges for children).

Tea: 2oz

TEA

Sugar: 8oz

*The amounts given are per person per week unless otherwise stated.

December 1941

Milk: 3 pints

(7 pints for young children and expectant mothers)

July 1942

Sweets and chocolate: 2oz

PURE DRIED WHOLE EGGS

DATES ITEMS BECOME FREELY AVAILABLE AGAIN

July 1948	Dec 1948	Oct 1952	Feb 1953	Mar 1953	April 1953	Sept 1953	May 1954	June 1954
Bread	Jam	Tea	Sweets	Eggs	Cream	Sugar	Butter, cheese and margarine	Meat and bacon

TEA

CREAM

SUGAR

NATIONAL BUTTER

Much more than just food

It was not just food that was rationed. Clothing and cosmetics had ration books (picture ②), as did soap and washing powder. Coal and gas were also rationed and people were told not to put more than 5 in (13 cm) of water in a bath to save on the use of coal for heating the water.

Because medicines were needed by those fighting, even medicines were in short supply at home.

Rationing grows

In January 1940 butter, bacon and sugar were the first things to be rationed (see page 35). Meat and jam were added in March 1940. Tea, margarine and cooking fats were added in July 1940 and cheese in 1941. Later, rice, condensed milk, breakfast cereals, biscuits and cornflakes were rationed.

Milk was in short supply because the most efficient use of land is to grow crops, not rear animals. Much land that would have been grazed was ploughed up and the number of animals reduced.

Milk was delivered using the traditional horse and cart because petrol was rationed.

▲ ② Clothing coupons.

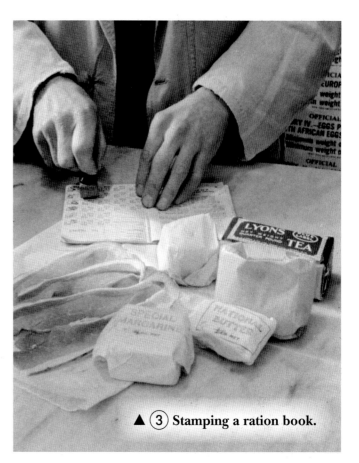

▲ ③ **Stamping a ration book.**

Queuing

Queuing was an important part of life for women. It took longer to serve customers as ration books had to be stamped, and many items were in short supply anyway (pictures ③ and ④).

If a shop suddenly had unrationed items for sale, the news would sweep around the neighbourhood and long queues would develop outside.

Queuing for food and other goods was so important that people would ignore air-raid sirens and carry on queuing to save losing their place in the queue.

◀ ④ There was very little choice of food. Most of it was called National Butter, National Flour, etc. Only a few items kept their brand names.

What did people eat during the war?

Because Britain cannot produce enough of the things it needs, it has to get them from other countries. In wartime, the amount Britain needed was kept low by rationing.

The Ministry of Food controlled food supplies through rationing. But it had another job. It had to make sure that people understood how to eat healthily because everyone had to work harder than before.

Food facts were published in the newspapers, shown in cinemas and also broadcast on the BBC radio.

Some forms of meat – rabbit, horse and chicken – were not rationed. But lamb, pork and beef were. Offal (liver, heart, kidneys) was never rationed and people could eat tripe (intestines) and pig's feet in jelly!

The range of foods in the war was much smaller than normal. But no-one went hungry and the rations made sure everyone had a healthy diet, with less fat and meat but more vegetables.

▲ ① One problem at the start of the war was that preserving food had become a factory process and the demands of war meant that factories were now used to make weapons. Fruit preserving centres were set up in schools to show people how to make jam from locally grown fruit. Sugar was supplied specially for this, then the jars were stored by the government.

Preserving food

This was a time before fridges were used, so any food grown at home that would not keep naturally had to be preserved in traditional ways, such as drying (meat and fish, eggs and milk), salting (meat, fish and cheese), pickling by putting in vinegar (onions and other vegetables) or boiling in sugar (jams). Many vegetables were best left in the ground until needed (carrots, potatoes, cabbages, etc).

▼ ② National rations: Because of rationing it was vital to know the minimum amount of food that was needed for a person to stay healthy. This was used to work out what the rations should be. You may like to find and weigh out the foods listed here.

A TYPICAL WEEK'S RATION FOR 1 PERSON IN 1942	
Bacon and ham	4oz (100g) Meat: To the value of 1s.2d (6p today) (perhaps a pork chop and four sausages). Sausages were not rationed but difficult to get; offal (liver, kidneys, tripe) was originally unrationed but sometimes formed part of the meat ration.
Cheese	2oz (50g) sometimes it went up to 4oz (100g) and even up to 8oz (225g).
Margarine	4oz (100g)
Butter	2oz (50g)
Milk	3 pints (1,800ml) occasionally dropping to 2 pints (1,200ml). Household milk (skimmed or dried) was available: 1 packet per four weeks.
Sugar	8oz (225g)
Jam	1lb (450g) every two months
Tea	2oz (50g) (half a packet or the equivalent of 15 tea bags)
Eggs	1 fresh egg a week if available but often only one every two weeks. Dried eggs: 1 packet every four weeks.
Sweets	12oz (350g) every four weeks

Pea pod soup

Today we might shell fresh peas and throw the pods away. But in the war the pods were used to make a pea pod soup. The pods were washed and placed in a saucepan with a chopped potato, an onion and parsley, or mint if available. It needed lots of salt and pepper to give it flavour (more salt than we would use today). It was brought to the boil and simmered until everything was tender. To make it more substantial, flour was added (about an ounce to each pint of soup). This also gave it a more creamy texture.

Sausage pancakes

Sausages and sausage meat were often easier to get than other kinds of meat. One recipe to vary how they tasted was to cook and mash potatoes, then add sausagemeat and mix it all up. It was then spread over the bottom of a frying pan and fried until golden brown.

If the leftovers from cabbage and other cooked vegetables were added, it was known as BUBBLE AND SQUEAK.

Vegetable oatmeal soup

1oz of margarine, 2 onions chopped, 2 tablespoons of oatmeal, a pint of water, lots of salt and pepper, half a pint of milk and three grated carrots. The oatmeal gave more body to this vegetable soup.

DIG FOR VICTORY

◀▼ ① *(Left)* Dig for Victory poster. *(Below)* School children helping to make an allotment in the garden of a bombed house.

Make the most of it

As rations became smaller, people had to find ways of coping. For example, if potato was added to flour, the flour would go further. Mothers made their own sweets, such as toffee from treacle. Two simple treats were bread and **DRIPPING** and bread and sugar.

If meat coupons were saved and mother was lucky enough to get a roast, she could have the roast on one day, then put some of it into a stew the next day, mince the meat for rissoles, and the remains could be made into **BUBBLE AND SQUEAK** for a fourth day.

Free school milk

From 8 December 1941 all children under the age of 2 were given supplies of free cod liver oil and blackcurrant juice. A small bottle of free milk was given at schools for all children. School dinners also started at this time. These were very important for the poorest people.

For a healthy, happy job

Join the WOMEN'S LAND ARMY

◀ ② Poster encouraging women to join the Women's Land Army.

Dig For Victory

To help make use of all of the land, the government launched a campaign called Dig for Victory (picture ①). The idea was to grow the food you (and perhaps your neighbours) needed in your garden or in your local park. London's royal parks, golf courses and tennis courts were all dug up. Soon nearly a million and a half families were growing vegetables.

Work on the farms

Women worked on farms, ploughing and doing the many other jobs that men had done before the war. These women made up the Land Army (picture ② and page 44). Children were also used in many ways to help harvest the much needed crops.

If people took a holiday, they often went to work on a farm. They could not go to the seaside anyway, for the beaches were closed and covered with barbed wire to prevent invasion.

Wartime Christmas

Christmas was a time of thinking about family members who might be away in the forces and also trying to be imaginative with rationed food and presents.

Christmas was a special time of the year, but it could not be the same as Christmases before the war.

- The blackout meant there were no lights in the shops or on outside Christmas trees (picture ②).
- Rationing meant that it was hard to make a good Christmas meal.
- Shortages meant that it was quite hard to get any kind of present.
- The war meant that many members of a family might be fighting overseas and so would be especially missed at Christmas.
- Evacuation might mean that you were spending Christmas away from your home.

Increased rations

The government tried to help in small ways. For example, in the week before Christmas, the tea ration was doubled and the sugar ration increased to 12 ounces.

▲ ① A party with children dressed as nurses, air-raid wardens or members of the armed forces. Notice all the children have cups of tea.

Practical gifts

People became very inventive about Christmas presents. Mums and dads might give each other a steel helmet or a leather gas mask case.

They might make presents such as by packing an old gas mask container with pouches made from old strips of cloth stuffed with straw. This could be used as a keep-hot box, so they could have a reasonably hot meal for lunch while at work.

▶ ② **Christmas in an Anderson shelter in the garden. Notice the corrugated iron roof. It must have been very cold and damp!**

In the early years of the war children received miniature Red Cross, RAF or naval uniforms (picture ①). New popular annual books appeared, with titles such as the *Blackout Book*.

Soap is most popular gift!

By the middle of the war Christmas gifts were gardening tools, bottling jars, seeds and bags of fertilizer, but the most popular gift was soap. Some parents gave National Savings books with a few savings stamps already added.

If mothers did want extra food at Christmas they had to start saving their ration coupons, or storing away unperishable food, months in advance.

If mums could get the wool, they could knit a pair of gloves as a present, or pull apart an old jumper and reuse the wool. A special treat for Christmas for children may have been a bag of sweets (which were on ration).

Home-made decorations

Many families made their own Christmas decorations by gumming pieces of coloured paper into chains or using any green bushes they could find. The Ministry of Food suggested:

"A Christmassy sparkle is easy to add to sprigs of holly or evergreen for use on puddings. Dip your greenery in a strong solution of Epsom salts. When dry it will be beautifully frosted."

43

In what other ways did the war affect people?

A war is a time of danger, both for the troops fighting it and for the people left at home.

People had curious feelings about the danger of bombing. If you were to have asked many people if they expected to die when the bombing started they would have replied that they never thought about it.

But people did get killed and so all children in cities would have seen more death than anyone today. Bombs might have fallen near to where they lived and they might have lost friends or relatives. Or the bombs might have fallen very close and destroyed part of their house, and even buried them in the rubble.

They may have lost everything they owned, or just been able to collect a few things from their damaged homes.

Worrying about the troops

Most fathers, many brothers and some sisters were in the forces and so there was always the worry that they might be injured or killed in the fighting. For much of the time people did not let themselves think of this, but the only contact was by the occasional **CENSORED LETTER** home.

▲ ① A propaganda poster in support of the women in the forces.

▼ ② Women working on a farm.

It was only when an official letter arrived at the house that some people had to face up to the awful experience of being told that someone they loved had been killed in action.

So people lost a lot that was dear to them, but they had to find the courage to keep going.

▼ ③ During the war, women had to do jobs that men thought only they could do, such as repairing railway tracks.

A new start

Most fathers were away in the forces, and many children did not see their dads for six years – until the end of the war. Mums had to take over many of the jobs that men had done, including working in factories and on farms (pictures ② and ③). They also worked in the forces (picture ①).

Before the war **CLASS** was very important. There were relatively few middle and upper class people and a lot of working class people. There was a big difference between classes, just as there had been in Victorian times.

Because everyone was in the same danger during the war, people were much more willing to help one another. Class began to drop away, for example, in the forces overseas as well as the Home Guard (page 30). The best leader might be from the working class and some of the ordinary soldiers might be upper class.

This made an enormous difference to the way everyone behaved and it would have a great effect on Britain after the war, too, bringing an end to much of the class system. Nothing after the war would be the same again.

Glossary

ABLE-BODIED Those thought fit for active service in the armed forces. People who had illnesses, disabilities or were under 16 or elderly, were not regarded as able-bodied.

ACK-ACK GUNS A common name for anti-aircraft guns. It mimicked the sound of the guns.

AIR RAID A sudden attack by bombing planes.

AIR-RAID WARDEN A person who looked after a neighbourhood, making sure that all residents obeyed the regulations for blackout and so on. They were a kind of special police force.

ALLIES A group of countries who have pledged to fight together.

BILLET The word was originally used to mean the lodging given to troops, often forcibly, during a war. It was extended to mean the lodging of children (also by order) as a result of evacuation.

BUBBLE AND SQUEAK Fried leftovers from previous meals, mainly potato and cabbage.

CENSORED LETTER A letter that has been read by a member of the armed forces with any information that might be of help to an enemy blacked out. This was done during the war so that, if a letter got into the hands of the enemy, it would not give away the position of the person who wrote it.

CLASS The way that people thought of themselves as belonging to different groups based on wealth and upbringing. There were upper, middle and lower (or working) classes. Upper classes were aristocracy, middle classes did not do manual work and received a regular salary, and lower classes did manual work and were paid for what they did (wages). It was a system much used in Victorian times.

CONCENTRATION CAMP A place where people were held without trial in often terrible conditions. In Germany during the Nazi times, concentration camps often included gas chambers where large numbers of people were murdered.

▲ Boys learning the skills to help them become airforce apprentices.

DICTATOR A single person who has total power to do what he wishes and who does not have to ask permission of, for example, a parliament.

DRIPPING The fat that dripped off the meat while it roasted. It cooled into a white, and very tasty, fat. It was a very concentrated form of food energy.

FIGHTER PLANES Small, very fast planes equipped only with machine guns. Their job was to shoot down the larger and slower bombers.

MEMORIAL A plaque or stone tablet put up to act as a way of remembering those who lost their lives in the war.

MERCHANT SHIP A ship designed for carrying cargo. Not a fighting vessel.

NAZI The letters in German stand for **NA**tionalso**ZI**alistische Deutsche Arbeiter-Partei: National Socialist German Workers' Party. The leader of the party was Adolf Hitler.

PROPAGANDA A way of changing the meaning of events and actions to suit the purposes of one group of people.

RADAR The letters stand for **RA**(dio) **D**(etection) **A**(nd) **R**(anging). A method of determining the location and speed of an object. Radar works by transmitting signals and measuring the time it takes for them to bounce off the targeted object and return.

RATION/RATIONING A fixed portion of food, coal, clothes, etc, allotted to civilians in times of scarcity.

SONAR The letters stand for **SO**(und) **NA**(vigation and) **R**(anging). It was a measuring instrument that sent out a sound (called a 'ping') in water and measured distances in terms of the time for the echo of the ping to return.

TORPEDO An underwater missile, launched from a submarine.

Index